HEALTHY·LIVING·

Talking About
The Dangers of Alcohol, Tobacco, and Caffeine

**By Alan Horsfield
and Elaine Horsfield**

Gareth Stevens
Publishing

Please visit our Web site **www.garethstevens.com**. For a free color catalog of all our high-quality books, call toll free 1-800-542-2595 or fax 1-877-542-2596.

Library of Congress Cataloging-in-Publication Data

Horsfield, Alan.
Talking about the dangers of alcohol, tobacco, and caffeine / Alan Horsfield and Elaine Horsfield.
    p. cm. — (Healthy living)
Includes index.
ISBN 978-1-4339-3661-6 (library binding)
1. Alcoholism—Juvenile literature. 2. Tobacco use—Juvenile literature. 3. Caffeine habit—Juvenile literature. I. Horsfield, Elaine. II. Title.
HV5066.H67 2010
613.8—dc22

2009043443

Published in 2010 by
Gareth Stevens Publishing
111 East 14th Street, Suite 349
New York, NY 10003

© 2010 Blake Publishing

For Gareth Stevens Publishing:
Art Direction: Haley Harasymiw
Editorial Direction: Kerri O'Donnell

Cover photo: iStockphoto

Photos and illustrations:
pp. 5, 6, 8, 9, 10, 11, 12, 14, 15, 17, 18, 19 (top and bottom), 20, 22, 23, 24, 25, 26, 27, 28, 29, 30 iStockphoto; pp. 5, 6, 7 (top), 25 UC Publishing; p. 7 (bottom) Georges Jansoone; p. 12 Photos.com; p. 14 Anthony Woodward; p. 19 (middle) Shutterstock.com.

Printed in the United States of America

CPSIA compliance information: Batch #CW10GS: For further information contact Gareth Stevens, New York, New York, at 1-800-542-2595.

Contents

What is a drug?

The word "drug" can mean any substance used to change the way the body works.

When swallowed or injected, a drug changes how the mind or the body works. If this change helps the body, the drug is a medicine. Medicines can be used to prevent or cure an illness. If the change harms the body, the drug is called a poison.

Drugs can be solids, liquids, or gases. All bring about physical and/or mental changes in the body.

I feel sick.

Me too!

Drugs

Prescription drugs are medicines prescribed by a health professional for treating an illness. These drugs are listed as legal by the government. They must be used as directed.

Illegal drugs generally fit into three main categories:

Depressants—drugs that relax you and cause sleep; for example, **alcohol**.

Stimulants—drugs that increase feelings of well-being. They increase energy and make you more alert. They can also make you feel more awake. Some drugs are made from natural products, while others are made from chemicals. Athletes use these drugs to boost their performance. **Caffeine** and **nicotine** are stimulants.

Hallucinogens—drugs that make people imagine things that are not real.

Don't be tempted to use illegal drugs. They are dangerous, their quality and ingredients are not monitored, and they may kill you!

legal drugs

illegal drugs

medicinal

nonmedicinal

prescription **OR** over-the-counter

alcohol
tobacco
caffeine

Over-the-counter drugs include such items as painkillers, eyedrops, mouthwashes, itch powders, cold formulas, and many ointments and balms. They are mostly used for minor ailments. Over-the-counter drugs can be bought in supermarkets and health food stores as well as **pharmacies**.

Prescription drugs can only be bought from a qualified pharmacist. Most pharmacies have a special prescription counter.

How drugs enter the body	Example
swallowed as solids	car-sickness pills
swallowed as liquids	cough medicine
injected	insulin for diabetes
rubbed on	ointment for cuts
dusted on	antifungal powder
breathed in	inhalers for asthma
sniffed in	allergy sprays

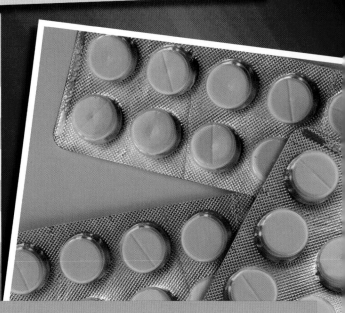

Asthma inhaler

Drug problems

It is possible for people to take a bigger dose of drugs than prescribed. Sometimes it is accidental and other times it is deliberate. Some people believe that taking more drugs than prescribed will help them feel better more quickly, feel less pain, or even feel happier. This is also true of people taking illegal drugs. Both prescription drugs and illegal drugs can create serious health problems.

• **Overdose.** This happens when too much of a drug is taken. The drug acts like a poison in the body. It can harm, and may even kill, the person.

• **Addiction** or **dependence.** This is when a person relies on a drug, legal or illegal, to such an extent that they find it very difficult to stop using it. Trying to stop can cause severe physical and/or mental pain.

Where do you get drugs?

Where do drugs come from?

Many drugs come from plants. Caffeine is found in coffee beans; nicotine comes from the **tobacco** plant. Humans have been extracting drugs from plants for thousands of years, and many of today's drugs are derived from plants. Many drugs today are also developed from nonplant materials, such as chemicals. These are called synthetic or artificial drugs.

Don't be tempted to use illegal drugs. You never know exactly what is in the drugs. Legal drugs are all tested to be safe for people if used as directed.

Medicinal drugs are not available from people other than pharmacists or people in the medical profession. If anyone else offers you a pill, medicine, or powder (other than your parents) say NO! It could kill you.

Drugs and schools and shops

Apart from a school nurse, first-aid teacher, or emergency worker, no one can legally give you a drug at school, in the shopping center, or on the way to and from school. You must say NO to these people if they offer you a drug. Tell your parents or teacher immediately.

Did you know?
A pharmacy is also called a chemist (shop) in Australia and New Zealand. In North America, it is a drugstore.

Before chemists, there were alchemists

Alchemy was a medieval chemical science. It was the skill of making useful potions from herbs and other plants. Potions were said to heal, increase agility and strength, produce a certain spell, or give protection from evil spells.

19th century Italian pharmacy

Apothecary is an old name for a medical person who prepared and dispensed medicines for doctors and patients. Now we call them pharmacists. Apothecaries often had a shop where they also sold tobacco!

What is so special about tobacco, caffeine, and alcohol?
These are drugs that are legal and can be bought without a prescription. These drugs can cause health problems. There is very little control of their purchase and consumption. Now you are ready to find out about tobacco, caffeine, and alcohol. READ ON!

7

Why is nicotine a harmful drug?

What is tobacco?

Tobacco is a plant with a broad leaf. It comes from tropical America. It is now grown in many countries all over the world. The leaves are cured (dried and preserved) for smoking. Tobacco contains a drug called nicotine. Nicotine is addictive. Tobacco products cannot be sold to people under 18 years of age.

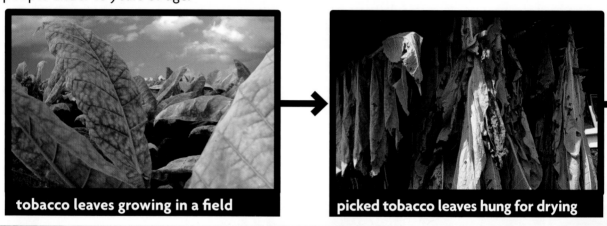

tobacco leaves growing in a field

picked tobacco leaves hung for drying

In 1492, Christopher Columbus first saw Native Americans using tobacco. At that time, people believed tobacco had health benefits.

Later, tobacco was introduced into Europe and the rest of the world.

Tobacco timeline

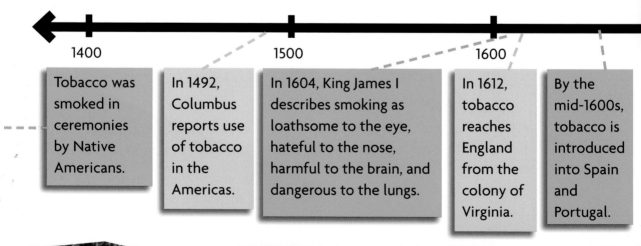

1400   1500   1600

Tobacco was smoked in ceremonies by Native Americans.

In 1492, Columbus reports use of tobacco in the Americas.

In 1604, King James I describes smoking as loathsome to the eye, hateful to the nose, harmful to the brain, and dangerous to the lungs.

In 1612, tobacco reaches England from the colony of Virginia.

By the mid-1600s, tobacco is introduced into Spain and Portugal.

What is nicotine?

Nicotine is in tobacco products (cigarettes and cigars). It is an addictive drug. It causes changes in the brain that make people want to use it more and more. It causes lung irritation. It also causes narrowing of blood vessels and increased blood pressure and heart rate. Nicotine affects the central nervous system.

The World Health Organization (WHO) estimates that, each year, five million people die from smoking-related illnesses. Within the next twenty years, smoking will cause more deaths than any other single disease.

Did you know?

Nicotine is used in some insecticides to kill insects. **Think about that!**

dried leaves are shredded to make cigarettes

There are over 4,000 chemicals in modern cigarettes, including cadmium (the black part in batteries), arsenic (poison), ammonia (in floor cleaner), and acetone (nail polish remover). Smoking even one cigarette is harmful to your body.

Native Americans made a solemn, sacred ceremony of smoking. As the peace pipe was filled, a prayer was said to the Creator, each of the four directions (north, south, east, and west), and Mother Earth and Father Sky.

an example of a Native American peace pipe

1800   1900   2000

In 1760, the first tobacco factory opens in Cuba. Cuban cigars are highly prized by cigar smokers. Tobacco is still an important Cuban industry today.

By the 1800s, tobacco use has spread to Asia and Africa.

By the mid-1900s, many people are aware of the health risks of smoking.

By the early 2000s, smoking is banned in most public places.

That took 500 years!

Is any tobacco product safe?

Regardless of how the tobacco is smoked, it is still dangerous to your health. Do not smoke!

A cigar is a tightly rolled bundle of dried tobacco, wrapped in a tobacco leaf. One end is lit. Smoke is sucked into the smoker's mouth through the other end. Cigars are just as dangerous to your health as cigarettes. **There is no safe tobacco!**

A cigarette is a tobacco product that uses finely cut tobacco leaves. It is rolled or stuffed into a paper cylinder. It is smoked the same way as a cigar. It is dangerous to your health.

Snuff is finely powdered tobacco that is sniffed through the nose. It was popular in the 1700s.

Tobacco is smoked in many different ways, none of which is safe. A hookah is a Middle Eastern smoking pipe, with a long tube passing through a bowl of water, which cools the smoke.

A smoking pipe consists of a small chamber (bowl) for burning the tobacco to be smoked and a thin stem (shank) that ends with a mouthpiece (bit).

The bowls of tobacco pipes are often made of wood, but other materials may be used.

Some tobacco facts

- Tobacco kills five million people a year worldwide. Half of these deaths occur in middle-aged people.
- Unless smoking habits change, about 650 million people alive today will eventually be killed by tobacco.
- Tobacco is the second major cause of death in the world.
- Smokers have shorter life spans and higher health care costs than nonsmokers.

Did you know?
Tobacco is the most widely grown nonfood crop in the world. It is grown in over 100 countries.

Fact

- Smoking is declining among males in most countries that have high standards of living.
- Smoking is increasing among males in most countries that have lower standards of living.
- Smoking among women is increasing worldwide.

Smoking will seriously harm your body!

Governments promote antismoking campaigns. Why? Because tobacco is poisonous and can be harmful to the body.

When so many people want to quit, what keeps them smoking?

Cigarettes and other forms of tobacco are addictive.

Nicotine is the drug in tobacco that causes addiction.

What are some of the health risks of smoking?

Heart disease is the biggest killer of smokers! Lung cancer and emphysema are also big killers of smokers. Emphysema is a lung disease that causes difficult breathing. But there are also many other problems associated with smoking.

addiction and withdrawal stress

smelly breath and smelly hair

eyes sting and water, need to blink often

blindness and cataracts

loss of sense of smell

smelly clothes

stained fingers

breathing polluted air

food has less taste

ordinary activities cause breathlessness

How do people get addicted?

Nicotine causes changes in the brain. The effect of nicotine is less dramatic than that of many other drugs. Despite this, nicotine addiction is as strong as, or even stronger than, some illegal drugs.

In large amounts, nicotine is poisonous. Smoking for the first time can make you feel sick and dizzy. After a while, however, the body gets used to nicotine and the smoker may want to smoke more.

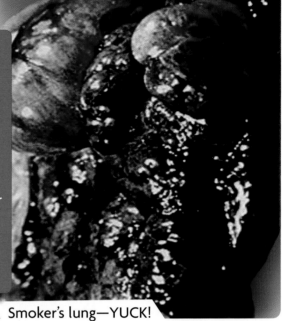

Smoker's lung—YUCK!

People with asthma who are exposed to smoke may have more asthma attacks.

Smokers have a limited sense of smell.

Smoking damages nearly every organ in the human body.

Smokers are at greater risk of developing cancer, especially in the throat and lungs.

Did you know?
Just one cigarette can reduce the blood supply to your skin for over an hour.

Q What's the result of smoking too much?

A Coffin!

*Active and **passive smokers** are at a greater risk of developing chest infections.*

*Smoking damages your **organs**, gives your skin more wrinkles, and lowers your fitness level. Say NO to cigarettes!*

Unless tobacco products are banned you have to make a choice—to smoke or not to smoke.

EPITAPH FOR BERNADETTE

Here lies silly Bernadette

Smoked too many cigarettes

Too late now to have regrets

R.I.P.

WHAT ARE THE HAZARDS OF SMOKING?

Cigarette smoking increases the risk of:

Mouth cancers
Optic neuritis (blindness)
Stomach ulcers
Unhealthy dry skin
Chest/lung infections
Nasty breath
Gum diseases

TASTE
ALS

SURGEON GENERAL'S
WARNING: Cigarette
Smoke Contains
Carbon Monoxide.

Yuck! What a stink!

Did you know?

About 90 percent of smokers started smoking when they were school age!

Did you know?

Each cigarette may shorten a smoker's life by 11 minutes.

Why not just quit?

Most smokers are addicted to nicotine, that is they are physically dependent on nicotine. Many smokers will only go an hour or two without smoking. A highly dependent smoker is one who smokes more than 25 cigarettes a day.

Even after long periods of not smoking, many smokers find themselves starting the habit again.

People smoke despite the harmful effects. Only half of smokers who suffer a heart attack manage to quit, despite advice from their doctor. Half of all regular smokers will die as a result of their habit.

Percentage of age groups who have smoked

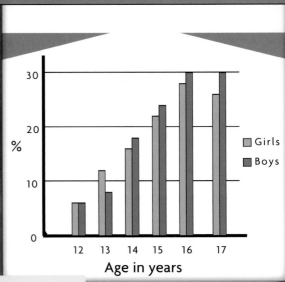

Nicotine strengthens the desire to smoke. It causes users to keep on smoking.

Two real-life stories

An addict's story

My name is Alex. I'm over 30 years old, and I have been a nicotine addict for more than half of my life.

I was 13 when I smoked my first cigarette. I got good at it. By 15, I was using my lunch money to buy cigarettes. I was not yet a slave to the habit. You couldn't tell me what was going to happen to me when I was old, or even what could happen to me with just a short time smoking. I was a teenager—and a cool one. When I started college, I could puff away in a small outside area set aside for smokers. I really enjoyed it! There are few smokers' areas these days.

On a return visit to my college many years later, there was a garden where the smoking area once was. New life now grows in the very spot where my fatal habit began!

The first time I tried to quit, I realized that I was addicted.

If you smoke, will you be able to quit? If you keep smoking, what will your health be like in 20 years?

Who gave you your first cigarette?
A friend stole it from his father!

Did you enjoy the experience?
Not really, but it looked tough! Like the Marlboro man.

Give a brief history of your smoking.
On and off in high school, and then heavier and heavier into adulthood.

What do you feel is the most likely cause of your smoking?
Mostly peer group pressure.

Can you give an estimate of how much you spent each week on cigarettes when you were smoking the most?
About $70. Cigarettes were cheaper then!

When did you first decide to give up smoking?
About 20 years ago.

What method or methods did you use to give up smoking?
Tried everything.

How long did it take and how difficult was it to give up?
In the end, it took about 10 days of going without. It was extremely hard.

Any comments you'd like to make?
Just don't start smoking! The longer you smoke, the harder it is to give up.

It is illegal to sell cigarettes to anyone under 18. When you reach the age of 18, you can smoke if you want to. But why would you want to risk your health?

What is passive smoking?

What is a passive smoker?

A passive smoker is a person who breathes in air that contains other people's smoke.

YUCK! That's like smoking when you're not!

If someone is smoking, the smoke they blow out can be breathed in by anyone who is near them. The smoker is actively choosing to breathe in this smoke. People nearby are passive smokers, also called secondhand smokers. Although they do not choose to smoke, they are breathing in the smoke released from a cigarette and the fumes exhaled by a smoker. Smokers do not consume all the harmful gases in a cigarette. They exhale some into the air around them where passive smokers breathe them in.

Cigarette smoke drifts silently and uninvited into places where it is not wanted.

Common excuses given by smokers

It's only the smoke seen in the air that is harmful.	FALSE: The cancer-causing matter in tobacco smoke remains in the air for hours.
It is okay for parents to smoke when children are not home.	FALSE: Furniture in smokers' homes becomes polluted with toxins. These toxins can be absorbed by people and become more harmful over time.
Rolling down the car window lets the smoke escape.	FALSE: Smoking in any vehicle is more toxic than in a house because it is a small, enclosed space. Opening a window doesn't get rid of all the smoke.
If children are healthy, passive smoking won't hurt them.	FALSE: Passive smoking can be linked to risks of bacterial meningitis, heart disease, and learning and behavioral problems.
Only children with asthma are affected by passive smoking.	FALSE: Passive smoking can cause asthma, but it has also been linked to bronchitis, pneumonia, and ear infections.
Children are safe as long as no one blows smoke near their face.	FALSE: Smoke can drift unnoticed, even in well-ventilated areas.

Did you know?

According to UK research, passive smoking at work kills three people every day. That's over 1,000 workers in the UK each year!

There are three times as many deaths a year from passive smoking at work in the UK as there are workplace accidents.

What is being done to make people safe?

Smoking is banned in all government buildings, on all public transportation (including planes, taxis, and buses), in many enclosed public places (cafés, hotels, and restaurants), and in the workplace.

Children beware!

Children who grow up in a home where one or both of their parents smoke have twice the risk of getting asthma and bronchitis, AND they are more likely to get allergies!

It's a fact!

Smoking stinks! Smoke makes clothes, furniture, and the insides of cars smell, as well as people's skin and hair.

What can you do about it?

- Move away from cigarette smoke. Leave the room if you have to.

- Talk to your parent about passive smoking. Remind them that in some states it is illegal to smoke in a car when children are there.

- Ask your parents to make the house and car smoke-free zones.

- Encourage (without nagging) any smoker in your family to give up smoking.

TO PASSIVE SMOKING LITIGATI
MOKING
TOTALLY
ROHIBITE
THESE

BREAKING NEWS!

Governments all over the world have begun to pass laws against smoking in a car when a child is present. Research shows that about 8% of new asthma cases are due to passive smoking.

Other smoking problems

Smoking in bed is a major cause of house fires, which can be fatal for an entire household. Tiny embers can smolder unnoticed and burst into flames. Smokers should make sure that butts are properly extinguished before placing them in garbage cans.

Many people think cigarette butts are biodegradable, but they are not. Furthermore, they contain many toxic chemicals. Because cigarette butts are small and light, they are easily blown from place to place or washed into waterways. Once there, the toxic chemicals leach out into the water. This makes the water dangerous for aquatic animals, the animals that eat them, and people as well.

littering

In February 2009, a discarded cigarette butt caused a forest fire in central Texas. The fire burned more than 400 acres of forests. This type of tragedy happens every year in the United States.

You can be fined for smoking in the wrong place.

FACTS ABOUT CIGARETTE-RELATED FIRES

- Fires caused by cigarettes kill 700 to 900 people in the United States every year.
- Property losses from smoking-related fires equal hundreds of millions of dollars each year.
- Mattresses, bedding, furniture, and trash are the most commonly ignited items in cigarette-related home fires.
- There were 30,400 cigarette-related home fires in the United States in 2006.
- About 25 percent of the victims of cigarette-related fire fatalities are not the smokers who started the fire. Thirty-four percent are children. Twenty-five percent are neighbors or friends. Fourteen percent are spouses or partners. Thirteen percent are parents.

Cigarette butts are carried through drains to the sea.

Young children can get burned if they play with matches or lighters. Lighters and matches should be kept secure under lock and key. They are not playthings.

Smokers can only smoke in open places.

They should make sure their butts end up in the provided ashtrays!

SMOKERS PLEASE

PLEASE NOT LITTER

Hey! What a great spot! Don't be a litterbug.

Where will these butts end up?

Yuck! Who might eat them?

The time it takes cigarette butts to degrade ranges from about two months to 12 years. Unlike paper, cigarette butts undergo chemical changes as they decompose. Within an hour of being in contact with water, a cigarette butt will start to leach toxic chemicals into the environment.

Tobacco advertising is aimed at you

Tobacco **advertising** can appeal to us in a number of clever ways. It might include misleading information and make us think less about the "bad" side of products. The ads appeal to us through:

Pride
Informed people only smoke when creative ideas are needed.

Intelligence
Buzzo Light Cigarettes contain just 5 grams of nicotine.

Fashion
4 out of 5 people insist upon smoking "Cool"!

Urgency
Hurry customers, only 5 Jumbo Cartons left!

Popularity
Opal Smoking means you'll never be without friends.

Ambition
Get the right job! Cigs will keep you calm through the interview!

Emotions
You'll be happier—do what you want! Enjoy "Just Smokes"!

A Free Gift
Buy Happy Smokes and enter a drawing to win a trip to Mexico.

Once, it was very stylish for women to smoke using cigarette holders. It didn't make cigarettes any safer!

In the past, cigarette producers tried to make sure their brand name was advertised everywhere. They wanted smokers to think of their product when they wanted to buy cigarettes. Now, advertising of tobacco products is not allowed in many countries.

Cigarette marketing

Scientific evidence shows that children remember cigarette advertising. Even though formal cigarette advertising is banned in the United States, advertising still exists on the Internet. It also exists in overseas sporting events which are reported or shown in the United States. Films, television shows, and computer games show people smoking.

Brand loyalty often begins with a person's first cigarette. Children who had smoked said their choice of cigarette brand was influenced by advertising, free samples, promotional items, package design, and the "health" benefits of low-tar and low-nicotine cigarettes.

Check out: www.tobaccofreekids.org
   www.time.com/time/nation/article/0,8599,1904624,00.html

Because smoking is the single largest preventable cause of early death and disease, some groups have initiated antismoking campaigns to educate people on the dangers of smoking. You have probably seen commercials by a group called Truth. They want people to know about the dirty tricks tobacco companies use to get people to start smoking. For instance, on the Truth Web site—www.thetruth.com—they reveal that between 1987 and 2005, tobacco companies increased their spending on advertising every year, reaching $250.8 million in 2005. Check out their Web site for more facts about the tobacco industry.

In the past, some tobacco companies produced flavored cigarettes that might appeal to younger smokers. Some have argued that flavored cigarettes are an attempt to get young people hooked on nicotine. They have been described as cigarettes with training wheels! Chocolate- and fruit-flavored cigarettes in brightly colored packaging are tempting to younger people.

On June 22, 2009, President Obama signed the Family Smoking Prevention and Tobacco Control Act. The new law gives the U.S. Food and Drug Administration (FDA) the power to regulate the manufacturing and marketing of tobacco. This law will cause great changes to the way cigarettes are packaged and marketed. For example, the cigarette packs will most likely have larger and more specific health warnings. It will also greatly prohibit any advertising that would target young people. In addition, the law prohibits the manufacture of flavored cigarettes.

21

Is alcohol a drug?

The drug found in beer, wine, and **liquor** is ethyl alcohol (or ethanol). Alcohol is produced by the fermentation of yeast, sugars, and starches.

Alcohol is in drinks such as beer, lager, cider, wine, spirits, and alcoholic soft drinks (alcopops). Alcoholic drinks have different strengths, which are measured as a percentage.

It is illegal to sell or supply alcohol to people under 21 years of age.

What does it mean to get drunk?

Getting drunk (**intoxicated**) is the result of drinking too much alcohol.

The word "intoxicated" comes from the word **toxic.**

"Toxic" means "poisonous": getting drunk means getting poisoned.

Drinking too much alcohol is a health risk.

Alcoholic beverages have been produced for over 12,000 years. The oldest alcoholic beverage was probably made from honey or berries. Winemaking was probably started about 6,000 years ago. The ancient Egyptians were probably the first to begin brewing beer.

Alcohol affects every organ in the body. It is a depressant that is rapidly absorbed from the stomach and small intestine into the bloodstream.

Alcohol is changed in the liver by enzymes. However, the liver can only change a small amount of alcohol at a time. This means the excess alcohol circulates throughout the body.

Brain function is impaired. This causes poor judgment, reduced reaction time, loss of balance and coordination, and slurred speech. The effect of alcohol on the body depends on the amount consumed.

Did you know?
The world's oldest known recipe is for beer!

What are the problems with alcohol?

Alcohol is related to high levels of harm and injury among Americans, some of whom are still in high school.

Alcohol problems for young people are often due to intoxication.

Problems include:

- being violent to others or being the victim of abuse
- alcohol poisoning and loss of consciousness
- being injured while playing sports or trying to perform everyday activities
- driving while drunk
- having problems coping with school or work
- having money problems because of the amount spent on alcohol
- getting into trouble with the police
- loss of control and harm to friendships

The more alcohol consumed, the greater the problems.

Drinking alcohol can result in:

- dilation of blood vessels, creating a feeling of warmth but causing a rapid loss of body heat

- increased risk of stroke, liver diseases, and some cancers

- coma and death, if alcohol is consumed rapidly and in large amounts

- damage to unborn babies if consumed by pregnant women

It's a fact

The Egyptians had a god of wine, Osiris, who was worshipped throughout the country. It was believed that Osiris also invented beer.

How is drinking bad for the health of young people?

Teenagers can be more vulnerable to the effects of alcohol because they have not built up a physical tolerance. They also lack drinking experience and are less able to judge their levels of intoxication. There is some new evidence that developing minds and bodies may be more at risk to the unwanted effects of alcohol. The earlier a young person begins drinking, the greater the risk of alcohol-related problems in later life.

Is all alcohol a drug? Where is it made?

Regardless of the type of alcohol or where it is made, it is a drug. All types of alcoholic drinks damage your health and affect your senses.

Some countries and their **traditional drinks:**

◆ Scotland (whisky)
◆ England (cider)
◆ United States (bourbon)

◆ Mexico (tequila)
◆ Jamaica (rum)
◆ Russia (vodka)
◆ Japan (saké)

◆ Germany (beer)
◆ France and Italy (wine)

Did you know?

Bourbon gets its name from a town in Kentucky. It was first produced by a Baptist minister!

I wonder which place port was named after?

Alcohol type	Produced from
wine	grapes
saké	rice
vodka	potatoes
gin	juniper berries
beer	hops
whisky	grains (barley)
rum	sugarcane

When consumed wisely and in moderation, alcohol is not a problem for most people.

What is prohibition?

Prohibition is any time during which alcohol is illegal. Prohibition has been tried in the United States, Britain, and Scandinavia. It still exists in many Muslim countries and some small communities. Such places are called "dry."

In the past, prohibition often led to an increase in organized crime as people were prepared to break the law to buy and sell illegal alcohol.

In the Wild West, the "saloon" quickly became a popular hangout among thirsty cowboys. Western saloons in television shows and movies usually have bat-wing doors, outlaws playing cards, and a lively piano player—not to mention the gunfights! Today, travelers can visit restored saloons in western tourist locations like Dodge City, Kansas, and Tombstone, Arizona. The saloon is an iconic remnant of a colorful era in U.S. history.

Bootleggers and Speakeasies

During the era of Prohibition in the United States (1919–1933), the Eighteenth Amendment to the U.S Constitution made alcohol illegal in the United States. This was seen as a way to reduce criminal activities and promote a healthy American image. The production and transportation of alcohol became known as "bootlegging." Many establishments continued to sell alcohol illegally. They became known as "speakeasies." Patrons could "speak easy" while ordering their favorite alcoholic beverage and not worry about being arrested.

Although they were illegal and were often raided by police, many speakeasies flourished during Prohibition. They were places where Americans could forget the worries of world wars and the Great Depression. However, most successful speakeasies were run by gangs and criminals. They could be very dangerous places. In 1933, the Twenty-First Amendment to the U.S. Constitution repealed, or reversed, the Eighteenth Amendment. The United States was no longer a "dry" nation, and bootleggers and speakeasies were no longer necessary.

Even though young people cannot legally purchase alcohol, they still see the advertisements for alcohol products. Alcohol advertising often tries to link drinking alcohol with well-known actors and attractive models doing fun things. Beer and wine advertisements often suggest that the product can make a drinker more relaxed and successful.

Love needs a good red spirit.

No "reality" advertising

Alcohol advertisements do not show the bad effects of drinking too much alcohol. The advertisements can give young people an unrealistic view of how alcohol will affect them.

However, there are rules set out by the government that regulate the advertising of alcohol. These rules try to make sure that the advertisements don't directly target young people or glamorize drinking alcohol in a way that unduly influences any young person who may see the advertisement.

It's a fact

It is estimated that the alcohol industry spends over $70 million each year on advertising their products. The rising costs of television, radio, magazine, and newspaper advertising has meant that advertisers have moved to popular, interactive media (digital TV, Internet, and e-mail), especially popular with younger people.

There have been recent developments of new styles of alcoholic drinks that are attractive to younger drinkers. These alcopop and alcoholic sodas are sweeter than spirits, wines, and beers. They are also packaged and promoted in ways that appeal to younger people. Alcohol producers deny that these drinks are designed to attract young drinkers, but studies show that such drinks are popular with underage drinkers.

These ads are promising something special if you drink their brand of alcohol.

What is it?

Is it real?

Can these promises be met by drinking?

Watching sports on TV is incomplete without a

SNUBBIES BEER

Waterfront Bar

Free Cocktails Friday Night 6–8pm

Enjoy the quiet and friendly atmosphere of the Waterfront Bar. Drop in for a drink and meet the girl of your dreams!

Alcohol marketing

The alcohol industry uses cutting-edge advertising and marketing techniques. There are rules for advertising, but the lawmakers have difficulty keeping up with the changes in technology.

The rules have been changed to cover advertising on the Internet. This does not cover advertising in games, video games, cartoons, and contests. Alcohol sponsorship of cultural and sporting events is still common.

Beer advertisements often suggest that the product can make the drinker more relaxed, happy, and successful. Advertisements for ready-mix drinks and alcopops often link the product with personal, social, and even business success.

Alcohol (and tobacco) companies are targeting children and teenagers with their Internet marketing. These companies use advertising techniques tied into interactive games that young people enjoy. Some companies are setting up Web sites in foreign countries to avoid advertising laws.

First sip is the best!

Caffeine is a drug

Caffeine occurs naturally in the leaves and fruits of certain plants. When people think of caffeine, they mostly think of coffee.

Caffeine is also found in tea, cocoa, cola soft drinks, and energy drinks. It is in chocolate bars, energy bars, and some over-the-counter medications, such as cough syrup.

Caffeine is found in:

the coffee bean

the tea leaf

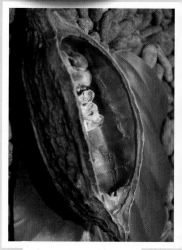
the cocoa bean

harvested coffee beans

dried and flavored tea leaves

Guarana is a climbing plant found in the Amazon region of Brazil. It is best known for its fruit, which is about the size of a coffee bean. Each fruit contains one seed, which has three times more caffeine than a coffee bean! Caffeine is a stimulant, giving a short, sharp boost to performance. It is widely used in sports drinks.

Q What are the most common things containing caffeine?

A Coffee, tea, cocoa, chocolate, and cola drinks

What does caffeine do to the human body?

Caffeine is a drug, which acts as a stimulant on the brain and nervous system. In small doses, it can make you feel refreshed and focused. In large doses, you are likely to feel anxious and have difficulty sleeping. Stimulants speed up the brain and nervous system.

It's a fact

Caffeine is the most commonly used drug in the world.

It is NOT illegal to sell or buy caffeine products.

Excessive amounts of caffeine cause:

- a rise in body temperature
- frequent urination and dehydration
- dizziness and headaches
- an even greater feeling of tiredness after the initial energy burst
- rapid heartbeat
- restlessness and not being able to sleep
- anxiety and irritability
- trembling hands

Did you know?

The easiest way to break a caffeine habit is to cut down gradually. This gives your body time to adjust to life without the drug.

My dad says coffee is not his cup of tea!

What does that mean?

Like many other drugs, it is possible to build up a tolerance to caffeine. This means people need to take larger doses to achieve the same effect. Over time, the body might come to depend on caffeine to function at its best.

Withdrawal symptoms can include tiredness, crankiness, persistent headaches, sweating, muscle pain, and being a grouch— for a while!

How much caffeine is too much?

How much caffeine is too much depends on your body size, your health, and how active you are. It also depends on how used to regular doses of caffeine your body is.

Approximate caffeine levels per serving

Caffeine product	Approximate levels per serving
Chocolate drink	30–60 mg
Instant coffee	60–100 mg
Espresso coffee	90–200 mg
Drip or percolated coffee	100–150 mg
Cola drinks	35 mg
Decaffeinated coffee	3 mg
Tea	30–100 mg (depending on the brew type and strength)
Energy or sports drinks	80–90 mg
Dark chocolate bar	40–50 mg per 2-ounce serving

Energy drinks

Many caffeine-containing energy drinks have about 80 mg of caffeine per drink. This is about the same as the amount of caffeine in a cup of coffee and about twice that in a can of carbonated, cola-flavored soft drink.

Did you know?

The International Olympic Committee classifies caffeine as a restricted substance.

Cafe

Generally speaking, 500 mg per day or less is considered an acceptable adult dose of caffeine for most people.

Pregnant women and athletes need to be careful about how much caffeine

Glossary

advertising	announcements designed to attract attention and interest
alchemy	the name for chemistry hundreds of years ago
alcohol	intoxicating drink that slows down reaction time and impairs judgment
brand loyalty	a longstanding decision to always buy a particular product even if similar items are available
caffeine	a stimulant found in coffee, tea, cocoa beans, and cola nuts
intoxicated	having lost control over behavior and movement from drinking alcohol
liquor	an alcoholic drink
nicotine	a drug contained in tobacco leaves
organs	body parts that have a special function
passive smokers	people who breathe in air that contains other people's smoke
pharmacies	places where drugs used for treating diseases are dispensed and sold
Prohibition	the period from 1919 to 1933 in the United States, when alcohol was illegal
tobacco	a broad-leaf plant that has leaves that are dried for smoking
traditional	having to do with behavior or beliefs based upon customs that have survived generations
withdrawal	a period after an addict stops taking a drug and suffers a level of distress

For Further Information

Books

Bailey, Jacqui. *Taking Action Against Drugs*. New York: Rosen Publishing, 2009.

Green, Carl R. *Nicotine and Tobacco*. Berkeley Heights, NJ: Enslow Publishers, 2005.

Ridley, Sarah. *Alcohol*. New York: Franklin Watts, 2010.

Web Sites

Drugs and Alcohol
http://kidshealth.org/teen/drug_alcohol/

DARE (Drug Abuse Resistance Education)
http://www.dare.com/kids/index_3.htm

Publisher's note to educators and parents: Our editors have carefully reviewed these Web sites to ensure that they are suitable for students. Many Web sites change frequently, however, and we cannot guarantee that a site's future contents will continue to meet our high standards of quality and educational value. Be advised that students should be closely supervised whenever they access the Internet.

Index